MW01036861

THE BETTER PASTOR

A Fable about Embracing the Role of Leading a Parish

Patrick Lencioni

Lighthouse Catholic Publishing
Sycamore, Illinois

The Better Pastor:
A Fable about Embracing the Role of Leading a Parish

Copyright © 2016 Patrick Lencioni

ISBN 978-0-692-58160-5

All rights reserved. No part of this book may be reproduced in any form without written permission from Lighthouse Catholic Publishing.

Printed in the United States of America.

Published by
Lighthouse Catholic Publishing
303 E. State Street
Sycamore, IL 60178

Book design by Stauber Design Studio.

To all of the priests in the world
who committed their lives
to serve God and to help others
know Him.

CONTENTS

INTRODUCTION vii

THE FABLE

Part I: The Conversation 3

Part II: The Work 45

Part III: Fast-Forward 75

TAKING ACTION

What's Next 97

Ideas and Suggestions 99

ABOUT THE AUTHOR 101

INTRODUCTION

THIS SHORT FABLE IS WRITTEN IN LOVE, gratitude and admiration for all pastors who have given their lives to serve the Lord and shepherd His people. The purpose is simply to provide new perspectives on how to lead those unique organizations that we call parishes. That's all.

The story is presented within the context of a pastor's most important role as spiritual father and shepherd, but I don't focus on a priest's faith or spiritual depth here. That is above my pay grade, as they say. My goal is simply to help pastors think about their "jobs" a little differently. I'm not prescribing a step-by-step model for running a parish. That would be a much longer book, one that would be difficult to write given the vastly different kinds of parishes out there. I'm simply trying to present a slightly new way of thinking.

Why do I believe I may have something to offer? For two reasons: First, my specialty is leadership and organizational effectiveness. I've spent the past twenty-five years helping leaders and organizations of every kind to eliminate frustrating roadblocks, politics, and dysfunction that prevent them from accomplishing what they might otherwise accomplish.

Second, I've had the blessing of spending the past decade or so working closely with the Catholic Church, most recently helping to launch something called The Amazing Parish movement. From pastors to parish staff members to bishops, I've had the opportunity to see the Church a little closer up than most lay people do, and to see the desire to better serve Christ that lives in Her. But I haven't gotten so close or spent too much time there that I've lost my perspective as an "outsider." I've found that while there is danger in trying to give advice to an organization without having knowledge about it, there is also a danger in knowing it too well and accepting its limitations in a way that only enables them to continue.

So I present this little book in humility and love for the Church. I pray to God that it helps you in some small way, because pastors may very well have the most important jobs in the world.

†

THE FABLE

PART I

†

THE CONVERSATION

UNSUSPECTING

As much as he enjoyed saying Mass in a full house on Sundays, Fr. Daniel Connor couldn't deny that he cherished the peace of the church in the evenings, when it was empty, barely lit, and quietly prayerful. Unfortunately, because of his hectic schedule and the seemingly endless demands on his time, he rarely found an opportunity to go there under those conditions.

So, on a Thursday night, he didn't mind having to walk the fifty-five yards from the rectory to look for his misplaced reading glasses, which middle age had required him to begin using recently.

As he approached the door to the sacristy, he had no idea that his parish—and his priesthood—was about to be changed forever.

ENCOUNTER

The last time Fr. Daniel remembered wearing his glasses was when he was reading the Gospel at Mass that morning, so he figured he'd start his search at the ambo.

As he left the sacristy and prepared to cross in front of the altar, he was suddenly startled when he noticed a solitary figure, a man, sitting at the end of the third pew in the darkened church.

"Oh, my goodness!" he blurted out. "I didn't see you there!"

Nervously, and to project a semblance of composure, he asked a follow-up question. "Is there something I can help you with, sir?"

The man stood and moved forward. "Hi, Father. I didn't mean to scare you."

As he came closer and into slightly better light, for a split second Fr. Daniel thought it was Robert Downey Jr., the actor. *Why would Iron Man be sitting in my church at five thirty in the evening?* he wondered.

A moment later he realized that it wasn't the famous actor at all, but a parishioner who only resembled him in poor lighting. And then Fr. Daniel began to panic because he couldn't remember the man's first name.

Normally, he wouldn't be too bothered about forgetting the name of a parishioner. No one could expect him to remember everyone. But this guy was the husband of Marie Hartman, one of the parish's most loyal and hard-working volunteers. The Hartmans had moved to the parish in the past year or so; they had three children in school, two of whom were altar servers. And they—the parents, not the children—had given a considerable amount of money during the capital campaign that had just ended.

Why can't I remember people's names better? Fr. Daniel lamented. He decided he'd have to fake it.

"Oh, hello there Mr. Hartman. I didn't recognize you in the dark. How are you?"

Mercifully, the man reminded his pastor. "It's Ken. Good to see you, Fr. Daniel." They shook hands. And then, as if to graciously let Fr. Daniel off the hook for not remembering his name, he explained, "I'm afraid that I haven't been around here as much as my wife. I've been traveling a lot for work lately."

Fr. Daniel was relieved by the subtle grace. "Well it's good to see you, Ken. How are Marie and the kids?"

"They're fine."

"Do you stop by the church regularly after work?" the priest asked.

"No. I work in the city and try to go to St. Cecilia's near my office when I'm not traveling. Today I just came by to see you."

Fr. Daniel was a little surprised. "You did? And you thought I'd be here in the church?"

"No, I just stopped by to pray for a few minutes before going over to the rectory."

Fr. Daniel took on a pastoral demeanor, assuming that Ken was having a personal problem and needed counsel, or even confession. "Anything particular you're praying for?"

Ken hesitated. "Actually, just for the intentions of our discussion. That I would have the courage to tell you the truth."

Fr. Daniel smiled. "Why don't we sit down right here then and talk? What is it that you need to have courage about?"

The two men sat in the first pew.

"Well," Ken suddenly seemed a little nervous, "it's not easy for me to give advice to a priest."

Fr. Daniel sat upright for a second, surprised. "Oh, this is about *me*?"

Ken nodded, and Fr. Daniel wondered if he shouldn't have come to look for his glasses after all.

CONFRONTATION

Ken Hartman explained himself. "The thing is, Father, I wasn't raised Catholic. In fact, I didn't go to church much at all as a kid. So I'm not sure what is an acceptable level of candor for someone like me to talk to you."

"Well, I think people should be direct with priests," Fr. Daniel explained without great enthusiasm. "But I guess it could depend a little on what you want to talk about."

Ken cleared his throat. "Right. Well, since becoming Catholic, I've been a parishioner at three other parishes. I've seen many of them struggle, and I've seen the pastors suffer. And I'm not proud to say that I haven't ever really tried to help. I've just sat back and watched things unravel, rationalizing that it wasn't my place to tell a priest how to do his job."

"Well, we can use all the help we can get." Fr. Daniel hoped that sounded more sincere than it was. Doing his best to delay what might be an uncomfortable moment, he decided to change the subject.

"Ken, remind me how long you and Marie have been here at St. Monica's."

"A little over a year now."

"And where did you come from?"

"We moved from the South Bay. I took a new job in the city."

Fr. Daniel was determined to postpone whatever advice was forthcoming as long as he could. "Oh, what parish did you attend down there?"

"Saint Mary's in Morgan Hill. I was on the parish council for a year, and Marie was a teacher's aide at the school."

Fr. Daniel lit up. "You don't know Fr. John Martin do you?"

Ken smiled and nodded. "Sure. He arrived just a few months before we had to leave. But we got to know him a little. He's a great priest."

"Yes, he is." Fr. Daniel agreed, though he quietly hoped Ken wasn't making that judgment in comparison to him. "Well, we certainly appreciate all you and Marie have done for us since you've arrived."

Though Fr. Daniel meant that, he was preparing himself not to like this man, who might be thinking that a big financial gift entitled him to tell his pastor what to do.

"Well Father, the church does so much for our family. We're glad to do whatever we can. I just wish I wasn't so busy at work lately so I could do more."

Fr. Daniel relaxed a bit, convinced that Ken was neither arrogant nor angry. *Maybe this conversation wouldn't be so difficult after all.*

He was wrong.

REALITY

Fr. Daniel continued to make conversation. "I'm sorry, Ken. Tell me what you do for a living. I know it has something to do with business, but Marie hasn't really explained it to me."

"For the past few years I've worked for a management consulting firm. I consult to executives and their leadership teams. Mostly strategy and organizational work. Before that, I ran a software company."

"Interesting." Fr. Daniel decided he couldn't delay the inevitable any longer. "So you have some advice for me?"

"Well, yes, I guess I do." Ken paused. "But I don't want you to think that just because we give money to the parish we have the right to tell you what we think you should do."

Fr. Daniel laughed and wondered if this guy was a mind reader. "No, don't worry about it. I appreciate that you're taking the time to share your thoughts with me." He was now feeling genuinely sorry for this accomplished professional who suddenly seemed like a fifth grader talking to a principal.

Ken began, a little more confidently. "Okay," he sighed, "I've been observing things around here for the past year or so, and talking to Marie about her experience volunteering at the parish. By the way, she's at home praying a Rosary for us right now."

Fr. Daniel smiled with genuine appreciation and relaxed a bit. "So what exactly do you want to tell me, Ken?"

"Well," he took a breath before continuing, "I guess I think there could be clearer management or leadership here at St. Monica's."

Fr. Daniel frowned, but not in an angry way. He was confused. "What exactly do you mean?"

"If what I gather is correct, I'm not sure there is a real plan for the parish. Or a vision."

There was a slightly awkward silence as Fr. Daniel just nodded while he considered what Ken had said.

Desperate to break the silence, Ken kept talking. "And I can't figure out who is part of your leadership team or how you make decisions."

More silence.

Finally, Fr. Daniel responded gently. "Well, I'm not sure you can compare a parish with the companies you consult to, Ken. We're not the same kind of organization."

"I realize that, Father," the consultant relented momentarily. "But you are an organization, right?"

"Yes, I suppose so. But we don't have a bottom line like a business. And things aren't as cut-and-dried in a parish as they are in most organizations."

Now Ken frowned. Confused. "Well, I also consult to nonprofits, Father. Help me understand how a parish is different."

"Well, even compared to a nonprofit, we're involved in so many activities that they aren't. Like sacraments. And the school. It's just not the same."

Ken wasn't convinced, and though he spoke with the same level of deference as he had just moments before, he didn't back off. "Father, I've worked with schools too. And they're certainly organizations. I'd have to say that I think a parish is definitely an organization."

Fr. Daniel didn't respond right away, and Ken continued. "In fact, there's really only one big thing that sets a parish apart from every organization I've ever worked with."

"What's that?" Fr. Daniel wanted to know.

"It's more important."

Fr. Daniel seemed pleased. He shouldn't have been.

THE HAMMER

Still as polite as ever, Ken followed up with a question. "Father, what is the ultimate purpose of a parish?"

Fr. Daniel thought about it for a second. "Well, ultimately, to save souls. To help people become disciples of Christ."

Ken nodded. "Right. And here's the thing: no organization I've ever consulted with has had any purpose or mission that was remotely close to that."

Fr. Daniel felt a sense of affirmation, especially coming from a man involved in the business world at such a high level. Which made Ken's next comment all the more powerful—and painful.

"And that's why I believe a parish should be better managed and better organized than any company."

Fr. Daniel couldn't argue with the logic of Ken's thinking, but he couldn't just sit there either. Trying his hardest not to sound defensive, he changed tactics. "You know, Ken, we didn't learn anything about leadership or management or strategy in seminary. And none of that was part of my calling to the priesthood. I became a priest to serve the Lord and, as you said, to bring people to Him."

Ken didn't respond right away. The look on his face demonstrated empathy and appreciation more than disagreement.

"I'm with you, Father. Your calling isn't about management and leadership. And I'm glad for that because what makes someone a great priest is his love for God and for people, not the ability to run meetings or do performance reviews."

Fr. Daniel was confused. *Is this guy suddenly agreeing with me?*

"But Father, you're not just a priest. You're a pastor." Ken paused to let that sink in. "You're not an associate, and you're certainly not a monk. You're the leader of this extremely important organization. And if you don't do that part of your job well, it affects the Church's ability to bring people to Christ. It affects people's lives."

Whoa. Fr. Daniel felt like a boxer on the ropes, defenseless to a barrage of truth. He threw a desperate punch. "But like I said, they didn't teach us any of this in seminary."

Ken smiled, kindly. "I understand that, Father. But you know something? Most of the CEOs I work with didn't go to business school."

Fr. Daniel seemed surprised. "Really?"

"That's right. Most of them studied English or psychology or computer science in college. Believe it or not, one guy I consulted to even studied theology. Then they found an interest in some field and started a business around it. A software company or a chain of restaurants or a construction firm. And that's when they had to figure out how to lead and manage their organizations if they wanted to make it."

"That's hard to believe."

"I know, but it's the truth. And even the ones who did go to business school didn't learn all the practical stuff they needed to run their organizations."

"So what did they do?"

"They became students of leadership and management."

Fr. Daniel frowned. "What does that mean?"

"It means they asked questions and read books and attended lectures here and there. They asked their peers for advice and they took advantage of friends and acquaintances who could teach them. They're constantly learning."

Fr. Daniel hesitated before asking the next question. "But what if they just like computers or food or construction, and they don't want to do the management stuff?"

"Then they get a job in that field and stay as far away from management as they can."

Now Fr. Daniel was deflated. He took a deep breath. "I don't know."

"You don't know what?"

Fr. Daniel just shook his head and after a moment repeated himself, "I don't know."

Ken smiled and tried to encourage his pastor. "Fr. Daniel, I think I've got a decent idea about you." He paused. "I can read people pretty well, and Marie is right."

Fr. Daniel seemed confused about where Ken was going with this.

"You have more than enough intelligence and interpersonal skills and intuition to be a leader." Ken paused again. "You just need to come to grips with the fact that it's a big part of your job."

Fr. Daniel didn't seem convinced, so Ken went on. "And you don't have to do it by yourself. There are more resources out there than you realize."

Fr. Daniel sighed. "But I don't know where I'd find the time. I'm swamped as it is."

Ken nodded, and didn't say anything. He wanted to honor Fr. Daniel's concern, and he felt like the priest might want to vent a little. Which he did.

"As it is, I barely have time to exercise. And that's when I start eating poorly. And it's not like I'm getting to bed at a good hour, between hospital calls and other things that come up, sometimes in the middle of the night. And then I'm up early in the morning unless I can find someone to do seven o'clock Mass."

Ken just nodded and didn't have to pretend that he was interested in what Fr. Daniel was saying, or that he felt for his pastor.

"I honestly don't think I have time to add more responsibilities to my life."

Convinced that the priest was finished venting for the moment, Ken dove back in. "I get it. That's what I hear from most of the CEOs I work with, too."

He paused to make sure that his empathy didn't seem trite. "But here's the thing, Father. You will actually save time by doing it. You will have more time to do many of the things that you wanted to do when you decided to become a priest. I promise."

Fr. Daniel suddenly seemed like he might be open to believing this man. He took a deep breath. "So this is the advice you came to give me, that I need to learn about leadership?"

Ken smiled. "It's actually just the first part."

"You mean there's more?" Fr. Daniel protested, humorously.

Ken winced, playfully. "Actually, I've got two more things for you."

TOUGH LOVE

Fr. Daniel took a long, deep breath and decided against trying to get out of the rest of the conversation. But a short break might be nice, he thought. "Do you want to go over to the rectory for the rest of this, Ken?"

Ken shrugged. "I don't know. I think this is a great place to talk, unless you think it's not appropriate."

"No, it's fine." Fr. Daniel smiled. "The closer we are to God, the better."

"That's what I was thinking." Ken chuckled. "And I need His help here, too. Like I said, I've never talked to a priest like this."

"Well, if you're worried about not being direct enough with me, I think you're doing fine."

They both laughed.

"Besides," Fr. Daniel said, "it can't get any harder, can it?"

Ken winced again. "I think it might."

Fr. Daniel seemed genuinely disappointed. "Really? What else am I doing wrong?"

Suddenly, Ken was worried. "Oh, I don't want you to think that I'm saying you're a terrible pastor or anything like that. Because I really do admire you, Father, and I appreciate the commitment you've made to your vocation and to the parish."

Fr. Daniel said, "But . . . ?"

Ken chuckled and then responded gently, "Well, I do think you could hold people more accountable."

Fr. Daniel didn't seem shocked, but he wasn't completely clear either. "Explain what you mean by that."

"Well, first you should know that this is something that most priests I've met struggle with. And for that matter, most CEOs and executives."

Fr. Daniel seemed to be just a little relieved to hear that, so Ken went on.

"Basically, it all comes down to this. When people aren't doing something well, they need to be told. They need to be held to a high standard."

Fr. Daniel frowned. "Maybe you could give me an example."

Ken didn't hesitate. "Well, let's talk about the music, for instance. Ten-thirty Mass."

The look on Fr. Daniel's face, the way he rolled his eyes and nodded, made it clear that he knew exactly where Ken was going, which made it easier for his parishioner to explain.

"So I'm guessing that you're as distracted on the altar as we are in the pews by the way the choir sings."

Fr. Daniel nodded with a mixture of reluctance and exasperation but didn't say anything.

Ken was suddenly excited. "Okay, so if *you* know they aren't very good, and if *we* all know that they aren't very good, the big question is, do *they* know that they aren't very good and that they have to get better?"

The priest let out a sigh. "What am I supposed to do? Maybe they're just not that talented."

"Oh, I think that's pretty clear." Ken responded sarcastically.

They laughed in a slightly guilty way.

Barely laughing now, Fr. Daniel put his head in his hands. "I don't even want to think about this."

"I know. No manager likes this part of his job."

After a few seconds Fr. Daniel sat up and, with an ever so slight sense of frustration, pushed back. "So, I'm supposed to just tell these people that they can't be in the choir?"

Ken responded with a question, one laced with mild sarcasm. "Is there someone else that you think should do it?"

Fr. Daniel was a little taken aback by his parishioner's tone, but resorted to humor. "I'll give you fifty bucks if you do."

They laughed again.

Ken, who was enjoying the conversation more than he anticipated, clarified his point. "Father, I'm not saying that you just go up to them and fire them. But if you don't let them know that something has to change, they'll keep doing what they do, thinking that it's good enough. And more people will start avoiding ten-thirty Mass."

Fr. Daniel suddenly sat upright, and the smile on his face disappeared. "People don't actually do that, do they?"

Ken nodded slowly.

"Really? They avoid that Mass?"

Ken took a breath. "My family does. Marie refuses to sit through it anymore."

Fr. Daniel winced.

Ken reached out and touched his shoulder. "It gets worse. If we find that the only time we can go to Mass on a weekend is ten thirty," he hesitated before finishing, "then we go to St. Peter's over in Pleasant Hill."

Now Fr. Daniel looked crushed. "It's that bad?"

Ken nodded. "It's really distracting to listen to them struggle. And it's kind of depressing to think that mediocrity is acceptable at St. Monica's."

Fr. Daniel closed his eyes. "Is that what people think?"

Ken paused. "Well, when a choir is allowed to continue forgetting the words to songs and singing out of tune, and nothing is done about it, how can they think anything else? Isn't that what you would think?"

Fr. Daniel was about to agree, but then he offered up a more ardent defense. "Listen, Ken, we pay the choir nothing. They're volunteers."

"So? Just because they're volunteers doesn't mean they get to do whatever they want."

Fr. Daniel sighed. "Sometimes it feels that way. I feel like I'm not allowed to tell a volunteer that they have to improve."

"You realize the problem that creates, right? It leads to a culture of mediocre volunteers."

Fr. Daniel nodded reluctantly. "You know, I'm pretty sure they'd just quit if they felt like I didn't appreciate them."

Ken pushed back. "You really think so? You think that if you told them that their singing distracts people and makes it harder for people to experience God at Mass, they might quit?"

Fr. Daniel shrugged as if to say *Maybe . . .*

"Well, if that's the case, then you should *definitely* tell them."

Fr. Daniel took a breath and replied with a strange mixture of kindness and exasperation. "That's easy for you to say, Ken. But then I'd have to figure out who else is going to sing at ten-thirty Mass."

Ken tried to be gentle. "And so you think it's better to let it be mediocre just to avoid having to deal with a different problem?"

Fr. Daniel hesitated, "Yes. I just don't need any more headaches right now."

Fr. Daniel knew that sounded lame, and Ken didn't pounce on him. He just sat there and let his pastor digest it all.

"Okay, Ken, what else is mediocre besides the choir?

Please tell me that's the biggest area that I'm not holding accountable."

Ken winced. "Sorry, Fr. Daniel. There are others."

Ken began. "For instance, there's the office staff."

Fr. Daniel seemed confused. "Can you be more specific?"

"Forgive me for being so direct here, but what about Mrs. Henderson?"

"What's the problem with Shirley?"

"You mean you don't know? She can be fairly . . . ," Ken searched for the right word, "unpleasant."

Now Fr. Daniel nodded and actually seemed relieved, as if he had been expecting something much worse. "Oh, sure. Everyone knows that. That's just the way Shirley is. But she's pretty efficient in her administrative work."

Ken was stunned by what he was hearing, but he remained calm and changed his approach. "So what exactly is Shirley's job?"

"She's the receptionist."

"And what does that job entail?"

"Well, most receptionists do the same things, right? Answer the phones, deal with various administrative tasks, give people forms to fill out. That kind of thing."

"So, if someone needs you to hear their confession, do they generally call the receptionist?"

Fr. Daniel nodded.

"And what about new parishioners? Who do they see first?"

Fr. Daniel seemed to know where this was going. "Shirley."

"What about parents thinking about having their children baptized, or wanting their kids to be confirmed, or needing to plan a loved one's funeral at St. Monica's?"

"That's Shirley, too."

Now Ken suddenly became just a little louder. "And you don't think that her being unfriendly is a problem?" He let the question hang there before continuing, even more incredulous now. "You realize, Father, that they wouldn't tolerate that kind of behavior at Chick-fil-A or Southwest Airlines. And they're just serving people chicken sandwiches and flying them from one place to another. So why in the world do you think it's okay at St. Monica's?"

Fr. Daniel was stunned into silence, convicted. After a few long seconds he calmly defended himself. "Do you know how long Shirley Henderson has been at St. Monica's?" He paused before answering his own question. "Nineteen years. That's seventeen years longer than I've been here. You don't just suddenly fire someone after nineteen years. I tried that once with a DRE in another parish and they almost hung me."

"Well, first, I didn't say anything about firing her. But before we even get into that, I think you need to ask yourself if parish employees are on the ministry team here, or if they're just part of a jobs program."

Ken sensed that Fr. Daniel felt the sting of the comment, but he decided to drive the point home further. "I mean, you said yourself that the purpose of a parish is to bring people to Christ. I'm guessing that involves reaching out to people who come to St. Monica's in search of peace in their lives, or finding ways to welcome new people here who don't already go to church. If Shirley isn't doing either of those things, then why in the world do you think you need to protect her? She's supposed to be ministering to others, not receiving charity."

Fr. Daniel just sat there for a long ten seconds with a blank look on his face.

Finally, he nodded. "Okay, I get that. But if you're saying I don't need to fire her, then what do you expect me to do?"

Ken responded passionately, "How about telling her that her job is really important? That she's on the front lines of the new evangelization? And that one of the most critical qualities she needs to have is being welcoming and warm and inviting?"

"And then what?"

"Well, then ask her if she wants to do those things, and she might decide that she doesn't."

"And what if she says she does want the job? I'm pretty sure she's not going to leave."

"Well, then let her know that you're going to hold her accountable for those behaviors. And then ask her if she thinks she can do that."

"Ken, do you really think she can change her behavior?"

Ken thought about it for a moment. "Probably not. But then again, I've seen more difficult people than Shirley change when they know they have to. Keep in mind, in nineteen years, no one has probably made this clear to her."

Fr. Daniel took another deep breath. "So let's just say she doesn't change."

"Then you let her know that you need someone in that job who is welcoming and helpful and friendly, and if that's not her, you'll have to find someone else."

Fr. Daniel rolled his eyes. "Oh, she'll freak out."

Ken shook his head. "No, not if you make it clear up front, and if you keep reminding her that she's not living up to expectations. In ninety-seven percent of the situations I see, people like Shirley either get better, which would be great, or they opt out on their own, which is the next best thing."

"What about the other three percent of the situations?" the priest wanted to know.

"That's when you have to take action, get the diocese involved, and maybe she will freak out. But you'll know it's for the right reason."

"That sounds awful."

Ken was now just a little frustrated by his pastor. "But it's not worse than what's happening now. I can't think of any way to justify letting her and the parish suffer like this." He paused before adding a final, painful comment. "That's not grace. And I certainly don't see it as being the kind of love that Jesus wants from us."

The priest was silent, just staring at his parishioner and then looking up at the large crucifix above the altar. Ken couldn't tell whether the priest was slightly angry or ashamed.

Ken continued, calmer now. "Father, do you think Shirley knows that she's not friendly? That people see her as rude and unpleasant?"

Defeated, the pastor turned back to Ken and admitted, "I don't see how she couldn't know."

"Okay, stay with me here, Father. If she knows she's not friendly, and I think you're right that she does, do you think she feels good about that?"

When the priest didn't answer, Ken continued. "Do you think she loves her job, Father?"

Fr. Daniel stared at Ken for a few seconds. "No. I don't think she's particularly happy."

"Don't you think it's time you sat down with her?"

Ken didn't wait for his pastor to answer. "Because the way I see it, you're allowing her to suffer in a job that she's not doing well, and you're allowing people in need to suffer through her unpleasantness and maybe turn away from the Church."

Fr. Daniel struggled to ask the next question. "Do you think we've actually lost people because of her?"

Ken didn't want to answer the question, but knew he had to. "Yes, Father. I know we have."

Sighing, he pushed for more information. "Tell me about it. Please."

"Well, Marie has told me a few stories."

The pastor hung his head.

Ken went on. "One couple came in to register as new parishioners. They asked about daycare during Mass, and Shirley practically scolded them for not being willing to bring their children to church and control them while they were there." He paused. "They left without taking the paperwork."

Fr. Daniel shook his head. "What else?"

"Well, I'm not exactly sure how much of this other story is, I mean, how this other one happened." He stammered. "I mean, Marie was a little uncomfortable sharing—"

Fr. Daniel interrupted, waving his hand for Ken to continue. "Come on, Ken. Just tell me. I need to know."

"Okay," he took a breath, "I guess Shirley openly criticized one of Marie's friends a few weeks ago for not putting more in the collection basket every week. This family is struggling financially. I guess Shirley made the comment sarcastically, probably even in an attempt at humor, but it was pretty awful for the woman." He paused. "That family is now going to St. Peter's."

Fr. Daniel turned toward the crucifix again, and just stared. For a full thirty seconds.

Ken sat in the discomfort of the silence, not knowing if he had gone too far.

Finally, the priest spoke.

"I have to tell you, Mr. Hartman." He paused for another five seconds. "That I'm not enjoying this conversation very much at all."

Ken felt scolded.

His pastor continued. "And I'm guessing that you're not enjoying it very much either."

Ken didn't need to respond.

Fr. Daniel finally turned back to look Ken in the eyes and said solemnly, "Which is why I need to thank you."

He reached out and shook Ken's hand. "It would have been easy for you to just go home after work today and write me off, to complain about all this with Marie and other frustrated parishioners."

Ken hadn't thought about it that way, but that is exactly what he would have done in the past.

Fr. Daniel continued. "But you came here to tell me the

hard truth, knowing that I could just push you away."

Ken had the faintest bit of moisture in his eyes.

With an intensity and sincerity that exceeded anything he had said thus far in the conversation, Fr. Daniel finished, "You have been a dear friend to me today, Mr. Hartman."

PUSHING ON

The ringing of Fr. Daniel's cell phone interrupted the moment. Removing the phone from his pocket, he looked at the number and explained, "Oh, I have to take this. Give me a moment."

Ken nodded, and Fr. Daniel stood and walked to the back of the church.

Ken took a moment to kneel and pray.

A few minutes later the priest returned.

"So where were we?" Before Ken could sit back down and answer, Fr. Daniel added, "I think we're all done, right?"

Ken seemed uncomfortable. "Well, actually, there's something—"

Fr. Daniel smiled and interrupted him. "I know, I know. There's one more thing."

Ken laughed, relieved.

"But before you move on," the priest said, "let me make sure I'm getting this right." Then he frowned. "I wish I had something to write this down on."

Ken smiled. "I'll send you an e-mail."

"Great. So, the first thing I need to do is take an interest in management and organizational stuff." He said it with no sense of dismissiveness. "And second, I need to confront people and hold them accountable when they're not doing a good job."

Ken nodded.

"So what's the third thing?" Before Ken could respond, Fr. Daniel added, "Are you sure you don't want to go over to the rectory for a coke or a glass of wine?"

Ken shook his head without hesitation. "No. This is definitely the right place for the last issue."

Fr. Daniel seemed concerned.

"But it's not a bad one. I mean, it's the least painful one of all."

The priest raised his eyebrows as if to say *Well, what do you know?*

"But it's probably the most important one."

Pretending to be discouraged, Fr. Daniel teased his new friend. "Oh, give me a break here, would you, Ken?"

Ken smiled. "Sorry, Father. But it's the last one."

"Thank the Lord for that. What is it?"

"Well, it's very different from the others. It's much more priestly and related to the entire parish as a whole, not just the management of the staff. And I could be wrong about this one, but I don't think I am. It has to do with something that is kind of personal, but—"

Fr. Daniel interrupted, joking, "Spit it out, man."

"It's about prayer."

"Prayer?"

"Yes." Ken paused. "I'd like to see you pray more."

Fr. Daniel sat back in the pew, and then he responded jokingly. "Wow. That *is* personal. Do you know something about my prayer life that I don't?"

Ken smiled. "No, I don't. And I think that's part of the problem."

Fr. Daniel was a little stunned. "What do you mean?"

"It's just that your prayer life is a mystery to me. And I'm guessing to most of the parish."

Still avoiding defensiveness, the pastor asked for clarity. "Are you saying that you have doubts about my faith?"

Ken held up his hands. "No, no. That's not what I'm saying at all, Father. It's just, I think it would be good for us to see you pray."

"What exactly do you think I'm doing at Mass?" Fr. Daniel asked politely.

Ken clarified again, "Well, I don't mean like that. Yes, we do see you pray at Mass all the time, and that's wonderful. I just think we need to learn more about how to pray, and that the best way to do that would be to learn about how you do it, and to do it with you sometimes. Does that make sense?"

Fr. Daniel thought about it. "So you're talking about personal, contemplative prayer?"

Ken nodded. "Exactly. I mean, I'm very curious as to what your daily prayer life is all about. I know I should just ask you, but most parishioners aren't going to do that. It seems too personal."

The priest laughed, "If there is one area of my personal life that people should probably understand, it's that."

"That's what I was thinking, too. And yet, how do we do that?"

A little relieved now that he understood what Ken was talking about, Fr. Daniel shrugged. "I guess you're right. That's not something most people are just going to come up and ask me about, even if I'd be glad to talk about it."

Fr. Daniel paused for a moment, and then he suddenly changed gears. "Forgive me for saying this, Ken, but this one sounds a little random. I mean, management I get. And as much as I hate the accountability thing, I see where you're coming from, as a management consultant and all. But prayer?"

Ken nodded. "I know. I was wondering the same thing myself. But I couldn't stop thinking about it. And after ten years of going to Mass and being part of a handful of parishes, the first time I ever really felt connected to the prayer life of a priest was a few months ago. And I can't tell you what a difference it's made."

"What happened a few months ago?"

WITNESS

Ken became suddenly excited. "So, I was at St. Cecilia's, near my office. I sometimes go to the noon Mass there."

"Yeah. You mentioned that earlier."

"Right. Well, I also occasionally stop by in the middle of the afternoon to pray when I have a break. After a while, I realized that Fr. Bartun, the pastor there, prays most afternoons at the same time. A handful of other people do too."

"They just pray silently?"

Ken thought about it. "Sometimes they say the Rosary or the Divine Mercy. And sometimes they just pray in silence. Occasionally someone will ask for a petition for their mother-in-law or for a coworker or for some war-torn part of the world. And then everyone just prays."

"How long does it last?"

"I don't know. I usually stop by for ten or fifteen minutes. But based on the times I've gone and seen them there, I'm guessing a half hour. Oh, and sometimes Father puts out the Blessed Sacrament. It's kind of like spontaneous Adoration."

Fr. Daniel scratched his head. "Don't get me wrong, Ken. I certainly appreciate what you're saying. But we have Adoration twice a week. I've added an extra hour of confession on Wednesday night, though people haven't really responded to that yet. And anyone can stop by the church here, like you did tonight, to pray."

Ken responded immediately and with enthusiasm, "There's just something extra special about seeing your pastor deep in prayer. I don't know how else to describe it. Seeing Fr. Bartun at St. Cecilia's has made me want to pray more, and it's even made me participate at Mass differently."

Fr. Daniel just looked at Ken, nodding, but still trying to digest what he was hearing.

Ken went on, "And now that I think about it, I actually think it made me want to come here and have this conversation with you tonight. Knowing that a pastor, deep in his heart, is desperate to bring people to Christ gives me the courage, even the moral responsibility, to do anything I can to help him. If more people understood this, I'm convinced it would change the way they prayed, lived, and even got involved in the parish."

The look on Fr. Daniel's face suddenly changed, as though it was starting to make sense.

Then his phone rang again. Looking down he said, "Excuse me," and answered it.

Listening for a few minutes, Fr. Daniel frowned. "Sure. When do you need me?" He paused, listening again. "Yes, I can be there in twenty or thirty minutes. Thanks."

After hanging up, he explained, a little distracted by the call, "I'm sorry, Ken. I need to go down to the hospital."

"No, that's fine. I think we're done here. I don't want to keep you any longer. Thank you for your time. I appreciate your openness and your—"

Distracted, Fr. Daniel didn't seem to hear Ken, and then he caught himself and interrupted. "I'm sorry. Did you just thank me?"

Ken nodded.

Fr. Daniel was suddenly incredulous. "Don't be ridiculous. I need to thank you for having the guts to tell me these things. I'm going to have to process it, and I'm not sure that I'll be able to act on it all. But I'm the one who should be grateful."

Then he hesitated.

"Ken, would you like to join me in a few minutes of prayer for an elderly woman named Beth who I'm going to visit at the hospital tonight? She's probably not going to make it through the weekend."

"Of course."

They knelt down. After about ten seconds of silence, Fr. Daniel began, "Dear Father, please grant peace and hope to Beth and her family during this time in their lives. Let me be a source of Your consolation. And thank you, Father, for bringing Ken into my life and the life of our parish. Bless him and his family. And help me to discern Your will as to the counsel he has given me. Make me humble and obedient always." He then prayed the Our Father and the Hail Mary, followed by another thirty seconds of silence.

Then he stood, shook Ken's hand and smiled, but a little sadly. "Thank you, my friend. Please give my best to Marie, and thank her for her Rosary tonight. I'm sure it helped."

The men genuflected and headed in different directions, Ken toward the back of the church and Fr. Daniel toward the altar to look for his glasses at the ambo.

PART II

†

THE WORK

ACTION

When the weekend came, the Hartmans decided to go to the five-thirty Saturday evening vigil Mass because they had another busy sports schedule with the kids on Sunday. They were glad to see Fr. Daniel coming down the aisle; even the kids usually enjoyed his homilies.

Fr. Daniel didn't notice them as he was processing toward the altar, as he was focused on preparing himself for Mass and singing the entrance song.

When he came to the lectern to read the Gospel, he saw Ken and Marie about halfway back, and he got a little nervous. As a result, his homily was a little shorter than he had planned, and he paid extra attention to the quality of the singing, hoping it wasn't a distraction to the Hartmans and everyone else. Fr. Daniel was thankful that Mrs. Garelli handled Saturday evening Mass. She was both a capable singer and had a reverence about her that fit nicely with the liturgy. Few people had ever complained about Mrs. Garelli.

After Mass, Ken and Marie looked for Fr. Daniel outside of church, but by the time they exited, he seemed to be gone. Though this was not customary for the pastor, the Hartmans figured he had somewhere to go. They didn't know that he had purposefully avoided them, going straight back to the rectory to be by himself.

For the next six hours, deep into the night and long past his normal time for bed, Fr. Daniel prayed, wrote, worried, and planned. Then he fell asleep at his desk.

GOING PUBLIC

THE NEXT MORNING AT EIGHT O'CLOCK Mass, Fr. Daniel changed everything about his homily.

"Today I'm going to talk about change. And humility."

He hesitated for a moment before beginning.

"In today's Gospel, Jesus challenges those who were going to stone a woman for committing adultery, explaining that anyone who had not sinned could throw the first stone. Of course, they dispersed, and that is the essential message of the Gospel, that we have all sinned and can condemn no one. But then he goes on to say to the woman, 'Go, and sin no more.' He doesn't say, 'Well, everyone is a sinner, so don't feel bad about yourself. I'm going to keep forgiving you anyway.'"

This provoked a few muted laughs from the people in the pews.

"Of course, God does keep forgiving us, but He expects us to do something about our sins. God's unconditional love is not meant to be a justification for complacency, whether you're a prostitute, a shoplifter, a gossip, or a lazy manager at work. Sin is sin, and acceptance of sin in any form separates us from God."

He paused before going on.

"And while some of us may be thinking about others we know in these situations, we must begin with ourselves. Yes, we are called to help one another avoid sin, but we're also called to take the plank out of our own eyes before we try to remove a splinter from our neighbor's."

Then he decided to be bold.

"And that applies to me as much as anyone else. Or perhaps in some ways more. And I'm standing here today to tell you all that I love being a priest, and I pray that I am a good one. But I'd also like to be a good pastor, and I can stand here and tell you all with some degree of confidence," he paused, "that I haven't been an excellent one."

A few of the people in the church were glancing at one another.

"I won't go into the details about how I came to that conclusion, but I'm convinced that it's true and that I want to do something about it. And while I'm not exactly sure what all this means and what I'm going to do, here's what I need from you."

He took a deep breath. The church seemed to take on a new level of silence.

"Starting tomorrow, I'm going to come to the church at seven thirty to pray each Monday evening, and I'd like to invite anyone to join me. You can come before the Blessed Sacrament to pray for the parish, for an improvement in my leadership of it, and for any other intentions you'd like to bring. I am determined to make St. Monica's an outstanding and amazing parish, and I know that I'm going to need great help from God. Thank you."

And with that, one of the shortest homilies he had delivered in the past two years, he led the church in the Creed and continued the Mass.

By the fourth and last Mass that evening, Fr. Daniel had mastered his talk after delivering it to more than twelve hundred of his parishioners. As a result, he felt more committed than ever to change his leadership and management of the parish, even if he didn't know where to start.

MONDAY NIGHT FOOTBALL

At seven fifteen on Monday evening, Fr. Daniel was finishing his dinner and watching the San Francisco 49ers struggle with the Seattle Seahawks in a much-anticipated game. Looking at the clock, he realized that he would have to miss the second half of the game if he was going to go to the church for his first hour of Adoration and prayer. *Maybe I should have picked a different night*, he wondered.

Turning off the TV and heading for the door, he decided that he'd be surprised if more than ten people would be joining him that evening, considering it was a game night and the short notice that he had given them.

By the time he arrived, he noticed that five of the regular older women of the parish were waiting for him. He thanked them for joining him, opened the church, and went to the sacristy to get dressed and make arrangements for Eucharistic Adoration.

Less than ten minutes later, as he left the sacristy for the altar, he was surprised to see more than thirty people filling the first ten rows of the church and a few scattered around the back.

An hour later, when he had risen to take the Blessed

Sacrament from the monstrance, he was surprised to see an additional fifteen or twenty people in the church, including Marie Hartman. *Maybe I've underestimated the hunger in this parish.*

OFF DAY

TUESDAY WAS FR. DANIEL'S DAY TO HIMSELF. Though he had in the past taken Mondays off, when he arrived at St. Monica's two years earlier, he had decided Monday was a good day to be in the office and talk about how everything had gone on Sunday. He even had a few staff members review his homilies. They had given him especially high marks for his brevity and clarity the past weekend.

After his morning prayers and Mass on Tuesday, Fr. Daniel headed for the nearest Barnes & Noble with a gift card in his wallet and his reading glasses in his hands. Making a brief detour to the on-site Café (the cashier insisted on paying for his mocha, explaining that her uncle was a priest), he went straight for the business section.

Twenty minutes later, Fr. Daniel had pulled from the shelves three books that looked interesting to him. One was about meetings. Another focused on having difficult conversations with colleagues and employees. The third was all about building a real leadership team. Finding a comfortable chair in a forgotten corner near the art history section, he settled in for the long haul.

After about an hour, it became apparent to Fr. Daniel that

he needed to take notes. Purchasing a notebook, a pen, and a highlighter, he went back to his chair and dove back in. At noon, he woke up, having drooled on his book about meetings. Grabbing some coffee and a sandwich, he returned for another four hours of reading. It was more focused studying than he had done since seminary and, much to his surprise, Fr. Daniel found it more interesting than he had thought it would be.

At four thirty, he was startled by a deep voice from behind one of the art history shelves.

"Hey priest man, I hope you're going to actually buy those books."

Spinning his head around to see who it was, he was relieved to see Fr. Miguel Mena, a pastor from Sacred Heart, a parish three towns to the north.

Fr. Daniel threw an empty coffee cup at his fellow priest. "You're early, knucklehead."

Fr. Miguel laughed. "My staff meeting was shorter than usual. And I'm starving. You ready for dinner?"

Looking at his watch, Fr. Daniel was stunned. "I had no idea it was so late. Wow."

"How long have you been here?"

Adding up the numbers in his head, "Almost seven hours."

Fr. Miguel laughed. "Wow. You're lucky they haven't thrown you out."

"Yeah, let's get out of here before they do."

After paying for the books, the brother priests headed for their favorite Mexican restaurant a block away.

PEER COUNSELOR

After ordering drinks and starting with chips and salsa, Fr. Miguel dove in.

"So, what's with the marathon library session?"

"I don't know. I decided that maybe I needed to learn something about being a leader."

Fr. Miguel nodded, neither disinterested nor fascinated.

Fr. Daniel kept the topic alive. "You ever do that?"

"What? Be a leader, or read books about it?"

"Study it. Learn about it."

Fr. Miguel nodded. "Yeah, I've got this guy in my parish who takes me to lunch every few months. He recommends books, lets me ask him questions about this and that. He's even led a few strategy sessions with my team."

"Do you understand it?"

"You mean the strategy stuff?"

"Any of it. Management. Strategy. Leadership."

Fr. Miguel nodded. "Yeah, most of it makes sense to me. I also look for stuff on the internet, and I've actually read a few books on leadership. Let me see what you've got there."

Fr. Daniel pulled the books out of his bag and handed them to his friend.

Spreading them on the table in front of him, Fr. Miguel nodded. "I've heard about this one on meetings. And I've read the teamwork book, which changed the way I think about what a leadership team is and who should be on it. Don't know the other one."

"Why haven't you ever mentioned any of this to me?" Fr. Daniel wondered out loud.

"You never asked. Why? Are you having a problem at St. Monica's?"

"No. Not really. I mean, nothing outrageous. But I had one of my parishioners mention a few things to me. Kind of rocked my world."

"This parishioner a troublemaker?"

"No, not at all. Great guy. Great family. Just wanted to help."

"Sounds like a blessing."

"Yeah. But it doesn't feel like one."

Fr. Miguel took a swig of his beer. "Humility is a pain in the butt, isn't it?"

Fr. Daniel laughed. "Yes it is."

"I'm great at humility." Fr. Miguel claimed, matter-of-factly. "Probably the best priest I know."

Fr. Daniel shook his head, smiling. "Yes, you are, aren't you?"

The priests were then interrupted by a third member of the clergy, a tall man with red hair and glasses, a few years younger than Miguel and Daniel.

"Sorry I'm late, guys."

Miguel stood and gave his friend a hug. "Great to see you."

Daniel reached across the table and shook the priest's hand enthusiastically. "How are you, Casey?"

"I'd prefer it if you would call me, Fr. Brennan." He joked.

"No problem, Casey." Daniel teased back.

The three friends finally sat down.

"What did I miss?" Casey wanted to know, grabbing a chip and loading it with salsa.

"We were just talking about leadership and management." Miguel pulled two of the books across the table and put them in front of the new arrival.

Looking at Daniel, Casey asked, "You guys aren't actually reading this are you?"

Daniel smiled. "I am."

Casey winced. "Sounds awful."

"I'm guessing you're not into it."

Casey laughed. "Listen, I didn't go to seminary to sit behind a desk and be a manager. That's not my thing."

Daniel gently challenged him. "So how do you deal with staff members and priorities and time management?"

Casey shrugged. "I do what everyone else does. I work too hard and I have my secretary protect me from things that I don't need to do."

"How does that work for you?" Daniel persisted.

Casey ate another tortilla chip and shrugged again. "God gets me through."

Now Miguel dove in. "Did you ever think that if you ran your parish better, and had a real group of leaders on your team, you could bring more people to Christ?"

Casey smiled but was a little less comfortable now. "Are you insinuating something about St. Bonaventure's?"

"No," Miguel smiled confidently. "I'm telling you straight up that if you're not leading your parish well, you're not fulfilling your duties as a pastor."

"Come on." Casey seemed to be asking Miguel to retract his statement.

"I'm completely serious, brother. I've learned the hard way."

Daniel wondered if Ken Hartman hadn't prearranged this conversation.

Casey wasn't ready to concede. "Listen, if this is so important, then why didn't they teach it in seminary? And how am I, one priest with a semi-retired associate, supposed to find time to be a leader and manager if I'm barely getting by right now?"

Now Daniel spoke up. "Did you know that most CEOs didn't learn how to be leaders in business school?"

Miguel and Casey seemed puzzled.

Daniel explained. "This guy in my parish told me that

most CEOs study something besides business, and that they learn the leadership stuff on their own."

Casey pushed back again. "Even so, where would I get the time?"

"That's what I always said," Miguel explained. "But I can tell you right now, in complete honesty, that I'm finding more time than ever to do what I became a priest to do, and that's because I'm starting to figure out how to manage and lead my parish staff."

Casey sighed and shrugged. "I don't know."

Daniel laughed out loud. "You sound exactly like I did last week when this guy confronted me about my bad management."

"Really? Someone did that?"

"Oh yeah. I hated it." He laughed again as Miguel gave him a supportive pat on the back.

Casey was suddenly more curious. "What did he say?"

"Well, he pretty much told me I had to take my job more seriously and start cracking down on people who aren't doing their jobs well. And that people were leaving the parish because they didn't think I cared about excellence."

Casey seemed incredulous. "He actually said that?"

"In so many words, yeah." Daniel suddenly seemed proud to have been rebuked.

"Is that why you have all these books?"

“Pretty much. And it’s why I spent the last seven hours at the bookstore reading them. I’m out of excuses.”

Casey shook his head. “Someone order me a beer.”

WEDNESDAY DRAMA

After morning Mass on Wednesday, Fr. Daniel spent much of the day in the parish office, observing. The combination of his talk with Ken Hartman, the dinner conversation with his brother priests, and the handful of ideas he had been reading about in the books he bought at Barnes & Noble, had already altered the way he viewed things. He was suddenly uncomfortable with many of the behaviors and attitudes he had been ignoring, or not noticing at all, for the past two years.

More than anything else, he noticed Shirley. Though she was something of a fixture in the office, no one who interacted with her ever seemed to be smiling. From the other women who volunteered in the office to the parishioners who stopped by for one reason or another, every interaction with Shirley was transactional, unemotional, and lifeless. It wasn't so much that she was always overtly rude; she just didn't seem to have any sense of joy.

Fr. Daniel felt a bizarre mix of emotions. He couldn't deny being frustrated at Shirley for not trying harder. He also felt bad that he, and the last three pastors before him, had let her flail in a job that she didn't seem to enjoy or do well. And he felt ashamed that he had let the parish suffer through all of that. He knew he had to do something about it, and sooner rather than later.

So before he could talk himself out of it, he asked Shirley to come into his office and closed the door.

"Shirley, I'm afraid that I should've had this conversation with you a long time ago, and I'm sorry that it has taken so long. That's my fault."

Now the small but stocky woman frowned, clearly confused. "Okaaayyyy."

Fr. Daniel stammered. "What I mean is, I'm responsible for creating a welcoming environment at St. Monica's, and I haven't been very intentional about that."

Still clearly confused, Shirley didn't say a word.

"Shirley, let me ask you a question. Do you like your job?"

Before she could answer, he clarified, "I mean, do you look forward to coming to work, and do you enjoy yourself while you're here?"

Shirley raised her eyebrows and shrugged. "Yes, I like my job. I like to get things done and stay busy. And I like to keep things from getting disorganized."

Fr. Daniel listened intently, and compassionately, seeing that his receptionist was starting to get a little nervous.

"Yes, I really appreciate you keeping things organized. I do. But what about the part of your job that deals with people?

Parishioners. Visitors. School kids and parents. Do you like that part of it?"

Hesitating, Shirley answered. "Sure. I like to help people with whatever they need. Why are you asking me this?"

Taking a deep breath and trying to smile in a way that was neither inauthentic nor patronizing, Fr. Daniel explained. "Here's the thing, Shirley. I think that while you work hard and get your work done, you don't give people the impression that they are welcome, or special. Do you know what I mean?"

Shirley seemed just a little confused, but not really surprised.

Fr. Daniel continued. "And I've never really sat down with you and explained that one of the most important parts of your job, or probably *the* most important part, is the way you deal with people who come into the office. You're the first person that people see or hear from when they call or walk in the door, and I would say that you can sometimes be—"

She interrupted him, smiling. "A witch?"

Fr. Daniel was caught off guard, and chuckled. "No, I didn't say that. I don't think that—"

Again Shirley interrupted him. "It's okay, Father. I know. I can sometimes be difficult. Even rude."

Just as Fr. Daniel was about to rejoice that the hardest part of this conversation was over, Shirley went on.

"But someone around here has to make sure that things

get done. And if everyone's just smiling and hugging and no one is making people do things by the rules, then this place will fall apart. Heck, Msgr. Wallace used to congratulate me for being the only one to keep people in line. He used to say that I did his dirty work for him."

And suddenly it all started to come together.

"Shirley, I am so glad that we're having this talk. Because it's easy for me to forget that I'm not the first pastor at St. Monica's."

"No you're not," the receptionist declared with a measure of relief and pride. "I've been here for almost twenty years, and I'd say that I know more—"

Now Fr. Daniel interrupted. "Just a second, Shirley. Before you go on, I need to make something clear. Though I'm not the first pastor here, I am the pastor now. And it's up to me to be clear about how we're going to do things."

Shirley was suddenly a little less comfortable again.

"And I don't want to punish you for doing things differently in the past, especially if other pastors encouraged you. But starting now, I want our parish office, and everyone who works here, to become ministers to the rest of the parish."

Shirley barely rolled her eyes, and Fr. Daniel decided that it would be better not to challenge her directly, but to stay on point.

"And that's why we're having this talk. I need to know if

being a welcoming minister is something you want to do. Because it's not for everyone. But it's also not optional."

The receptionist seemed a little unsettled now. "So what are you saying?"

Fr. Daniel smiled warmly. "I'm saying that everyone deserves to enjoy their work, and your work is going to change. I don't want to make you miserable. It's up to you to decide if you want to do it."

"Do you think I can?"

"I think that with God, all things are possible."

"Oh come on, Father. Don't give me that. Do you think I'd make a good warm-and-fuzzy receptionist?"

"Well, if you think I'm looking for someone who is fake, then that's not what I'm saying. But I think that if a person has a heart for people looking for Jesus, and they have some organizational skills, they can love this job. It's really up to them. Or I should say, you."

"I'm not going to lie to you, Father. I don't like this conversation. I feel like all the years I've been here don't matter."

Fr. Daniel walked around the desk and sat in a chair next to Shirley. "I'm sorry if I gave you that impression. I am so grateful for the commitment and effort you've given to St. Monica's for so many years."

She seemed relieved.

"This isn't about you. It's about what we need in this job.

And let's pray that you'll know if it's what you want to do."

Shirley nodded and rose from her chair to leave. "Okay. I'll do that."

"No, Shirley. I mean right now."

"Excuse me?"

"I want to pray about it right now."

Shirley looked more uncomfortable than ever. "And then I have to decide right away?"

Fr. Daniel laughed kindly. "No, no. I just want us to pray about this together."

She sat down, and Fr. Daniel lowered his head and asked God to bless Shirley and guide her in her decision, and to help her know how much God loved her. Then he said the Our Father, a Hail Mary, and as he made the Sign of the Cross he looked up to see tears streaming down Shirley's face.

He reached out to her and she continued to cry. "I feel like no one likes me and that I've been horrible."

Fr. Daniel put his hand on hers. "Shirley, we all feel like that sometimes. And that's what is so amazing about mercy and forgiveness. We are meant to be merciful and forgiving with one another just as God is with us. Don't think that you aren't appreciated and loved here, and that you can't make up for anything you might wish you hadn't done."

She nodded and cried a little more.

"And please forgive me for not having coached you around this earlier. I was a coward. Will you forgive me?"

She nodded. "Father, if I don't think I'd be a good receptionist, is there something else around here I could do?"

Whoa. Fr. Daniel didn't know what to say. "Well, I'm sure there is, but let's take that as it comes."

She continued, "You know, I don't do this job for the money. I mean, I need a little extra cash. But mostly I just don't want to stay home by myself. Even if there were a volunteer job I could do, that would be better than nothing."

Fr. Daniel was surprised by what he was hearing. "Well, here's the thing, Shirley. Whatever you or anyone else does here, it has to be done with a heart of ministry. You know what I mean?"

She nodded, a little sadly.

"And I can tell you right now that you can develop a heart for ministry. I know it's in there."

She nodded again.

"But running the reception desk might not be the perfect place for you. We'll see."

Shirley took a breath. "You know, I think I'd rather deal with poor people who have real problems than with moms who want to complain about the length of the Confirmation program or the congestion in the parking lot."

Fr. Daniel laughed. "I know what you mean, Shirley. I do.

But even those moms have real problems. And I don't think it's really about the Confirmation program or the parking lot."

She rolled her eyes again, but jokingly, and they both laughed.

"Thank you, Father." She began to wipe her eyes. "I'm sorry that I got so . . ."

"That's okay, Shirley. I'm really glad we talked."

Recovering herself, she moved toward the door.

Fr. Daniel finished the conversation. "Call me anytime if you need to talk. And know that you're loved here. Let's reconnect in a couple of days to see how you're doing. Okay?"

She sniffled, nodded, and left the room.

As the door closed, Fr. Daniel said a quick prayer of thanksgiving and thought to himself, *Maybe I can do this job after all.*

FELLOWSHIP AND ACCOUNTABILITY

THE INTERACTION WITH SHIRLEY prompted Fr. Daniel to call Fr. Miguel to tell him about the breakthrough and the hope it had given him. As it turned out, Fr. Miguel was wrestling with a similar situation on his own staff that he had yet to address, and he was grateful for the courage it gave him to hear about his friend's success.

And that's what prompted him to say something that would have a profound impact on their priesthoods—and their parishes.

"You know something? We should get together and talk about stuff like this more often. I'm guessing that there are a hundred other situations that we've faced that we could help each other with."

Fr. Daniel jumped at the chance. "I'm in. I know I need someone to talk to who isn't in my parish, but who I can be honest with. And who will tell me when I'm being a jerk."

Fr. Miguel laughed. "I'll look forward to that."

"We should ask Casey if he wants to be part of this."

Fr. Miguel hesitated. "I don't think he's into it."

"That's why he needs to come. Why should we let him or

his parishioners suffer?"

"But if he's not interested or thinks it's a waste of time—"

Fr. Daniel interrupted his brother priest. "Then he probably won't show up, or he'll stop coming after a while. Either way, I think we have to try."

"You're right. Let's do it."

They agreed to combine it with their already scheduled semi-monthly dinners, but to extend it to a full three hours to give them ample time for detailed discussions. And they agreed to meet in places outside of their parishes that were quiet and private enough to have substantive and confidential conversations.

It would be the best decision they had ever made, outside of becoming priests.

PART III

†

FAST-FORWARD

TWO YEARS OF LABOR PAINS

The next two years would be messy, wonderful, difficult, and transformational for Fr. Daniel and St. Monica's. The first critical step in the journey, one that preceded all the other changes, was the establishment of a real team to run the parish. Looking back, he knew that he could not have accomplished even a fraction of what was achieved had he tried to lead the parish the way he had always thought of doing it: alone. Not that he hadn't always appreciated staff members and volunteers; it was just that for years he believed that the pastor was supposed to be the one who made all the decisions—to be the carrier of the leadership cross, so to speak.

Fr. Daniel quickly realized that although he was ultimately responsible for the parish, and all accountability for what happened there came back to him, he did not need to shoulder the burden of decision-making, management, and leadership by himself. In fact, doing so was not only hurting the parish but also diminishing the joy of his vocation.

So after discussing it with Fr. Casey, Fr. Miguel, and Ken Hartman, Fr. Daniel decided that he needed a small group of people whom he could trust, and who would have the maturity, capability, and humility to help him transform St. Monica's.

He was able to identify those people fairly quickly, settling on his head of business operations, director of religious education, liturgy coordinator, and associate priest. Between the five of them, they could manage the staff and lead every aspect of parish life. The problem would be dealing with the staff members who would not be part of that group.

Four staff members were initially upset by not being included in Fr. Daniel's new team. But after hearing him explain the reason for the change and the responsibilities of the group, two of them quickly understood the rationale and were thankful not to have that burden. Two others were not so malleable.

One of them, a long-time parishioner and director of music, was irate. He felt that his tenure and profile warranted being included on any team at the top, even if his interest and expertise were limited to music. Fr. Daniel had a gentle yet direct meeting with him about the situation, and was disappointed when it did not go as well as had his conversation with Shirley the receptionist (who was now happily working in the St. Vincent de Paul food pantry).

The other disgruntled staff member was the finance manager and accountant. Though she technically worked for the head of business operations, she had grown accustomed to being involved in Fr. Daniel's twice-monthly, all-staff meetings where she reported on weekend collections and guarded budget allotments with her life. Not being part of the top team was unacceptable to her.

Over the course of a few long weeks, the dissatisfaction of these two employees made the atmosphere in the office tense and unpleasant for everyone. Fr. Daniel started to wonder if forming the leadership team was such a good idea after all. No matter how hard he and the other members of the team tried to explain the reasoning behind the change, and that the team was not about power and prestige but responsibility, both staff members dug their heels in hard. And worse yet, they talked to other parishioners about their unhappiness. The situation only began to resolve itself when two things happened.

First, the director of music announced that he was taking a similar position at a neighboring parish, prompting some members of the staff to question Fr. Daniel's plan. Worse yet, a small but very vocal group of parishioners wrote him a slightly nasty letter expressing their concern about losing a parish icon who had been singing at St. Monica's for almost fifteen years.

On the advice of Fr. Miguel, Fr. Daniel met with them and listened patiently to their concerns, and then he explained that the changes he was making were for the long-term good of the parish. And then, with humility and confidence, he explained that some people who didn't like the changes might opt to go elsewhere, and that would be okay. Only two parishioners actually left. Fr. Daniel couldn't deny in his heart of hearts that he was glad for their departures, even if one of them was a relatively large donor.

The finance manager was a different story. She wasn't going to quit, but she wasn't showing any signs of letting go of her disappointment. After discussing the matter with the team, Fr. Daniel did one of his least favorite things in the world: he let her go. Though this didn't provoke any minor revolts among the parish at large, a few staff members and volunteers were shaken.

Fr. Daniel would later describe this time as "the dark period." And he would credit Ken Hartman and his weekly breakfast conversations for helping him avoid backpedaling. Thankfully, the dark period came to an end sooner than the leadership team expected.

Within a month of their departures, morale in the parish office and among the music ministers had improved immensely. Fr. Daniel came to learn that the attitudinal problems of the former employees had not been limited to the recent situations, but that they had been stirring minor discontent for years. To Fr. Daniel's surprise, there was an unexpectedly profound sense of relief in the office, even among a few of the staff members who were initially upset by the changes.

And when new employees were brought in who better fit the culture and direction of the parish, whatever remnants of concern about the departures seemed to dissipate completely. Still, Fr. Daniel made it clear that he would not allow unkind remarks to be made about the former staff members, and he led prayers for them at subsequent meetings for the next two months.

One of Fr. Daniel's biggest concerns was how the parish council and finance council would react to his new team and approach. He hoped that they wouldn't feel alienated, so he sat down with each of them to explain not only what he was doing, but also how he had come to the decision to do it at all. He even brought Ken Hartman to help him. At first, there was some initial concern. But after explaining the importance of having a management team, and his own frustrations with managing his own time, energy, and pastoral joy, both councils came to the understanding that the new approach would allow them to better focus their efforts on oversight and advisory input, rather than doing administrative legwork and fighting fires.

Of course, while all this was going on, Fr. Daniel and his team were busy learning to work together. They immediately started having weekly meetings, working hard over the course of the first six months to make those sessions more focused and productive. They openly discussed personnel issues in the parish beyond their own areas of management responsibility, and critiqued one another's programs and ministries with an increasing level of grace and candor. Most surprising of all, they sometimes argued, even stepping over the normal lines of courtesy from time to time. When that happened, they simply apologized and moved forward. And of course, through all of it, they prayed together. For the parish. For the team. For one another.

Less than a year after establishing the new and smaller team, every member would say that it was the best work experience they had ever had. And the most painful. But it was worth it.

One of the first and most critical accomplishments that came out of the team was the creation of a real plan for the parish. Not an ethereal, lofty-sounding paragraph about being all things to all people, but a compelling and actionable plan for making St. Monica's an outpost for evangelization and discipleship in the community. A big part of arriving at the content of that plan was reading two great books about parish life written by pastors, *Rebuilt* and *Divine Renovation*. Though neither matched exactly what was happening at St. Monica's, each book provided invaluable insights and perspectives that would prevent Fr. Daniel and the team from reinventing the wheel and experiencing unnecessary pain.

As for the changes to various ministries and programs, Fr. Daniel and the team found that it was rough going at first, as people resisted letting go of the way things had always been done. He quickly learned that by going back to the parish plan and looking at everything in light of evangelization and discipleship, potential arguments about cutting this or adding that turned into productive discussions around what would bring people to Christ most effectively. And whenever he began those conversations with prayer, something that he had not done often enough in the past, hearts and minds opened to God's prompting.

Eventually, more and more people among the staff and in the parish were able to make changes in their areas without a great deal of supervision, as they all used the parish plan as a guide, and prayed in the same way that Fr. Daniel and the other leadership team members modeled.

Still, there were challenging times, brought about by economic stress and diocesan requests that sometimes came about at inopportune times. But by relying on fervent prayer, tapping into the entire leadership team, and sticking to the simple plan, Fr. Daniel was able to avoid the sense of frustration and isolation that he often felt before. And that kept his team, and the employees and volunteers they managed, on track as well.

Throughout the transformation at the parish, Fr. Daniel

continued the breakfast meetings with Ken and the dinner sessions with Fr. Miguel and Fr. Casey. More than once, the priests closed down a restaurant as they went deep in discussing, brainstorming, and praying about how to solve a thorny issue in one of their parishes. The perspective they gained from one another, and the support they relied on to do difficult things was, as they often said, beyond measure. They often marveled at how they had survived without that level of support before.

By the end of the second year of the transformation at St. Monica's, almost everything about the parish seemed different and new. By sharing responsibility with his leadership team and giving the parish a sense of clarity about the vision and plan, Fr. Daniel was now enjoying his ministry as a priest more than ever. He was exercising more, eating better, sleeping more regularly, and, most important of all, administering the sacraments with a greater sense of joy. And for that he was profoundly grateful to God.

As for Fr. Miguel and Fr. Casey, they had somewhat different experiences based on the unique challenges and opportunities that they inherited in their parishes. But because the three friends shared a common new vision of their roles, and because they helped one another throughout their journeys, the end result of their labors was more similar than they could have predicted. Most important of all, each parish was being run by a team, and with a greater focus on bringing more people to Christ and making them disciples.

After two years, the three priests had become closer friends than before and felt a real sense of responsibility to one another's parishes. They shared resources, filled in for one another during vacations and illnesses, and even agreed to divide some programs so that each could specialize in areas of strength and send parishioners to different parishes for various programs and services. A few parishioners in each parish even chose to start attending one of the other parishes, which was uncomfortable at first. Eventually, the three priests came to see it as an opportunity for their people to find the place that best met their needs.

FIRST FRUITS

Though every aspect of St. Monica's had been impacted, the most noticeable change could be seen on Sundays. Without tampering with the liturgy, Fr. Daniel and his team had improved just about every part of the experience of going to Mass at the parish.

While homilies had always been pretty good, now they were more actionable, consistent, and crisp. Fr. Daniel and his associate, who had been assigned to the parish a year into the transformation, spent more time preparing for their weekend talks, coordinating their messages with one another, and soliciting candid feedback from trusted staff members before and after the weekend presentations. Fr. Daniel noticed that parishioner comments after Mass had become far more focused on the specifics of his message rather than just the generic "nice homily" remarks. And many of those comments continued throughout the week, when school parents or other parishioners stopped by the rectory to tell him how his words had impacted the decisions they made that week.

Music at St. Monica's had improved significantly, too. Most noticeably, far more people were singing at Mass, and in a worshipful, prayerful way. This was due to three factors.

First, the various musicians and cantors started working together to pull from the same list of songs, even if those songs were presented in different styles. This allowed more parishioners to learn the words. Second, the songs were chosen to better complement the Mass, either by accentuating what was happening on the altar at a given time, or by reflecting the message of the Gospel and other readings. Third, Fr. Daniel had a difficult talk with one of the most enthusiastic singers at the parish, who also happened to be one of the worst. Like he had done with Shirley, he walked into a dangerous situation and, within weeks, had transformed a bad singer into a fantastic proclaimer of the readings. It was a win-win intervention, one that Fr. Daniel never would have attempted in the past.

Though he certainly didn't change the nature of the Eucharistic celebration at all, Fr. Daniel actually found a way to make it even more dramatic for parishioners. The key was contrast. While he insisted that the beginning of Mass be more welcoming, that the readings and the Gospel and the homily be delivered with more clarity and passion and joy, when it came to the consecration, he decided he would go in an entirely different direction.

In order to draw attention to the beauty and centrality of the Eucharist, Fr. Daniel would have the lights in the church lowered significantly, and then he would remind people about the awesome miracle that was about to take place on the altar. He would then use austere and poignant music to highlight the reverence of the moment. Of course, there was no substitute for his own reverence or the sincerity and passion of his words during the consecration.

Parishioners commented that the reception of Communion had taken on greater depth for them, and that the Mass had become more emotional, both in its energetic moments and contemplative ones.

Finally, the welcoming atmosphere at Masses had improved substantially, and with far less organized effort than Fr. Daniel and his team had expected. Some of this came about through more formal training of "greeters" who were not just older parishioners handing out song sheets and bulletins, but people of all ages actively reaching out to parishioners, especially newcomers. A bigger part was Fr. Daniel and his associate asking any new attendees at Mass to raise their hands, and then reminding everyone to take personal responsibility for welcoming those people not only into the parish but into their lives as well.

The new approach to hospitality did have its detractors. A few parishioners complained that they weren't comfortable being a church diplomat, so Fr. Daniel simply encouraged them to find other ways to minister. A few long-time parishioners argued that some new people might not want to be welcomed, that perhaps they came to Mass and preferred to be anonymous. Fr. Daniel resisted his urge to disagree with them and defend the initiative. Instead, he just smiled and kindly let them know that those people probably wouldn't raise their hands. But he went further, confidently explaining that being more welcoming was going to be the new approach at St. Monica's, and that it would be okay if some people who preferred a more docile culture chose to go to another parish. Complaints subsided within the first few weeks.

But St. Monica's transformation went far beyond the weekends. On virtually every night of the week, the church parking lot—which was also used as the school playground—was mostly full. From Bible study classes to youth groups to small group programs, most of the conference rooms, classrooms, and gymnasium spaces were being put to use. And the people running those sessions were almost never staff members, but rather parishioners themselves.

What made the parking lot situation particularly amazing was that none of the cars were there for basketball practice. That's because Fr. Daniel had decided to let a neighboring parish be the host site for CYO basketball, a program that was popular but not effective in helping people grow in their faith. Though he had been tempted to keep CYO and try to improve it, his team convinced Fr. Daniel that monopolizing the gym and parking lot would prevent the growth of other disciple-making activities that were central to the parish's new focus. Thankfully, they had been right. Even the most vocal—and tall—parents who had bemoaned the end of CYO on campus would later admit that the trade-off was a good one. Still, as Ken warned him might happen, a few parishioners decided to leave.

As proud as Fr. Daniel was of the weekend and weeknight activities that took place on the parish grounds at St. Monica's, it was the culture of the parish at large that amazed him the most, and the central part of that culture was prayer and fellowship. From the parish office to the carpool lanes at school to the homes of the parishioners themselves, there was a new level of energy and activity around matters of faith and love and discipleship.

As Fr. Daniel looked back at the process of those two years, he was amazed at how it came about, and how God's grace had flooded him in the good times as well as the difficult ones.

GRATITUDE

Almost every facet of Fr. Daniel's priesthood had been affected in some way by the transformation at St. Monica's. Even the last five minutes of his day.

Before going to bed, after his regular nightly prayers, he thanked God for restoring his joy as a priest and a pastor—and for bringing Ken Hartman into his church that evening. He prayed for his staff members and volunteers, and for all those involved in ministries and activities in the parish. And he prayed for those who lived in St. Monica's parish boundaries, including those who had not yet been reached.

In addition to all that, Fr. Daniel prayed for his friends Miguel and Casey, and for the people in their parishes. More than any time since becoming a pastor, he felt a strong connection to the larger Church, to the body of Christ that lived and breathed beyond the boundaries of his parish.

Fr. Daniel had never felt such joy in his calling, and for the first time he understood that his vocation was something more than simply being a priest, as beautiful and sufficient as that was. He was also a pastor. And every night he thanked God for allowing him to understand the special beauty in that vocation.

TAKING ACTION

WHAT'S NEXT

I HOPE AND PRAY THAT THIS SHORT STORY has provided you with some measure of new insight or motivation for embracing your critical, difficult, and wonderful role as a pastor. If so, it's important that you do one thing right away.

Something.

That's right. The most important thing is that you not set this book aside with the intention to think about it later. Instead, take some specific action, *right now*, to address an area that resonated with you from the story.

To make that easier, I thought it might be helpful to briefly recall what Fr. Daniel learned from Ken, Fr. Miguel, and his own experiences. Here is a summary of the various lessons highlighted in the story.

- A pastor is not just a priest but the leader of an organization that requires management and leadership skills.

- Part of leading an organization is holding people accountable for excellence, which often involves difficult, uncomfortable, and loving conversations.

- A pastor needs a real management team to do all of this. He can't do it by himself.

- A pastor needs support from "outsiders" and other priests.

- The Mass, which is the source and summit of the faith, is the most visible sign of the health of a parish. Excellence in the celebration of Mass encourages parishioners and visitors to become more involved and to go deeper in their faith and in the parish.

- Parishioners, volunteers, and staff members want and need to understand their pastor's depth of faith. Being a competent and inspiring manager, as important as it is, is not enough.

- Leading a parish to become amazing is hard and takes time. It will involve pain, suffering, opposition, criticism, and great humility. Trying to avoid these things will lead a pastor to back off and accept mediocrity.

- Prayer is always the answer. The most important part of all this is praying and enlisting others to pray for and with you for God's guidance and blessing in doing His Will.

IDEAS AND SUGGESTIONS

HERE ARE A FEW IDEAS AND SUGGESTIONS for going deeper in transforming your parish.

- FIND SOMEONE TO HELP YOU. One of the best things you can do is sit down with someone else—another priest is a great idea, but it could be a staff member or friend—and talk about what you learned in this book and what you'd like to do. Get someone else involved who can encourage you and hold you accountable.

- EXPLORE THE AMAZING PARISH WEBSITE. Please visit *amazingparish.org* where you can download free resources and discover how to implement many of the ideas mentioned in this book.

- READ GREAT BOOKS. Another good idea is to go out and get one of the many books written specifically for, and sometimes by, parish leaders. These include *Rebuilt: Awakening the Faithful, Reaching the Lost, and Making Church Matter* by Fr. Michael White and Tom Corcoran; *Divine Renovation: Bringing Your Parish from*

Maintenance to Mission by Fr. James Mallon; *Becoming a Parish of Intentional Disciples* by Sherry Weddell; and *The Four Signs of a Dynamic Catholic* by Matthew Kelly.

- Pray and enlist others to pray. And finally, ask your friends and parishioners to pray for you and with you to become the pastor that God wants you to be. Remember that growing as a pastor is a lifelong journey, and that God will be with you through it all.

ABOUT THE AUTHOR

PATRICK LENCIONI is a *New York Times* best-selling author and president of The Table Group, a firm dedicated to helping organizations become healthier and more effective. He is a lifelong Catholic who, after more than twenty years in business, decided to spend more of his time and energy serving the Church. He is a cofounder of The Amazing Parish Movement (*amazingparish.org*), committed to helping pastors and their teams improve organizationally and spiritually. He has worked with a host of parishes, schools, and dioceses, and has consulted to a wide variety of Catholic apostolates.